THE GIRL WHO LEARNED HOW TO KNEEL

Visit our web site at
www.stpauls.us
or call 1-800-343-2522
and request current catalog

The Girl Who Learned How to Kneel

The Story of Etty Hillesum

Patricia McCarthy

ST PAULS

Illustrations by Brother Michael O'Neill McGrath, OSFS
Bee Still Studio, www.beestill.org

Short selections from throughout the book, *An Interrupted Life:
The Diaries of Etty Hillesum 1941-1943* by Etty Hillesum.
English language translation copyright © 1983 by Jonathan Cape, Ltd.
Reprinted by permission of Henry Holt and Company, LLC.

Library of Congress Cataloging-in-Publication Data

McCarthy, Patricia, 1944-
  The girl who learned how to kneel: the story of Etty Hillesum /
Patricia McCarthy.
    pages cm.
 ISBN 978-0-8189-1359-4
 1. Hillesum, Etty, 1914-1943. 2. Catholic converts–Biography.
3. Christian converts from Judaism–Biography. 4. Hillesum, Etty,
1914-1943–Religion. 5. Holocaust, Jewish (1939-1945)–Netherlands
–Amsterdam. 6. Westerbork (Concentration camp). I. Title.
 BX4668.H49M33 2013
 940.53'18092—dc23
 [B]

                        2013007141

Produced and designed in the United States of America by the
Fathers and Brothers of the Society of St. Paul,
2187 Victory Boulevard, Staten Island, New York 10314-6603
as part of their communications apostolate.

ISBN 10: 0-8189-1359-2
ISBN 13: 978-0-8189-1359-4

© Copyright 2013 by the Society of St. Paul

Printing Information:

Current Printing - first digit	1	2	3	4	5	6	7	8	9	10

Year of Current Printing - first year shown

2013	2014	2015	2016	2017	2018	2019	2020	2021	2022

For

Jack

A brother who always stood tall

CONTENTS

Introduction ix

Chapter One
  Confusion 3

Chapter Two
  Kneeling 7

Chapter Three
  Daily Life 11

Chapter Four
  Suffering 17

Chapter Five
  Prayer 23

Chapter Six
  Jasmine 29

Chapter Seven
  Faith 33

Chapter Eight
  Transformation 39

Chapter Nine
  Final Thoughts 45

INTRODUCTION

Etty Hillesum was a Dutch Jew during World War II. In 1942, she was working for the Jewish Council around the corner from the Amsterdam house where Anne Frank was hiding. Anne was barely a teenager; Etty, a woman in her late twenties. Anne died from typhus in Bergen-Belsen in 1945 at 14 years of age; Etty was gassed in Auschwitz in 1943 at 29. Each left behind a diary – Anne's covered the two years she was in hiding, 1942-44; Etty's began in 1941 and ceased with her deportation to Westerbork in 1942.

Anne's legacy is that of a young girl who refused to give up hope in the innate goodness of people even from the midst of an unbearable reign of prejudice-fueled terror. Etty left us a profound journey from a youthful and tumultuous search for meaning in sex, philosophy, psychology and relationships, through an unexpected compelling sense of God's call, into the consummation of faith in mysticism. She grew to know God as ever-present lover of her and of all people. Her fierce intellectualism and radical need for personal fulfillment surrendered to a child-like simplicity leading to that complete abandonment which becomes absolute freedom and universal love. While Etty's outside world crashed around her, moving from fear of annihilation to the experience of it, her inner world discovered a calm and peace that nothing or no one could shake. Etty became God-intoxicated while Hitler continued his Jew-obsessed genocide.

Little is known of Etty Hillesum's early life. She was born in the Netherlands on the 15th of January 1914. Esther was her real name. Her mother Rebecca was a Russian immigrant who had fled a pogrom. Etty's father was a professor of classical languages. Etty lived in a family of high spirits and education. Her brother Mischa was a gifted pianist who played Beethoven publicly at the age of six. Her brother Jaap discovered a new vitamin when he was only seventeen and eventually became a medical doctor. Etty herself took a law degree from the University of Amsterdam, became a scholar of Slavic languages and was studying psychology when the war interrupted her education. All the Hillesum family perished in the concentration camps, except Jaap who died on the return trip to Holland after the camp was liberated.

History gives us the desperate, violent picture of Europe during Etty's life, but her diary leaves

Introduction

a legacy of hope and resiliency of spirit beyond imagination. During the sixteen months of her diary writing, from March 9, 1941 to July 3, 1942, life for the Jews in Holland descended into chaos. Holland capitulated to Hitler in May of 1940. In February 1941, the isolation of the Jews began. Employment was limited for them; homes and property were confiscated; ghettos were set up. By April of 1942 the deportations to Westerbork began. From there, most were moved to Auschwitz and their deaths.

Etty worked for the Jewish Council, a deceptive ploy concocted by the Germans to organize the Jews. The Jewish members of the Council thought they could control and protect their people from the Nazis. In retrospect, all they really did was provide order and information for the German extermination machine. Etty was among the first to go to Westerbork; she volunteered herself to spare another person. She remained in Westerbork from August 1942 to September 1943 when she was transferred to Auschwitz. She died there on the 30th of November 1943.

Etty's diary ends with her deportation to Westerbork. It gives the inner life of a searching soul, a woman deeply involved with her times and her people, a woman discovering God and reveling in that profound, seductive intimacy. In the short period of time which her diary covers, Etty reveals the steps she took to follow this God who seemed to be pursuing her at every turn in the road. At one point in her diary Etty talks about a growing desire to worship, to kneel. She begins to practice kneeling in the bathroom, the only place she could be alone without embarrassment from her prayer attempts.

"And there is God. The girl who could not kneel but learned to do so on the rough coconut matting in an untidy bathroom. Such things are often more intimate even than sex."[1]

"A desire to kneel down sometimes pulses through my body, or rather, it is as if my body had been meant and made for the act of kneeling. Sometimes, in moments of deep gratitude, kneeling down becomes an overwhelming urge, head deeply bowed, hands before my face."[2]

She herself said that if a book were to be written about her, it should be called: "The Girl Who Learned How to Kneel." I hope there will be many books about this extraordinary young woman. I accept Etty's suggestion for the title. Through her, I have learned again and again how to kneel and how to surrender to a loving God in the details of the day.

THE GIRL WHO LEARNED HOW TO KNEEL

CONFUSION

Etty's diary begins at a traumatic and unsettling time of her life. She is twenty-nine, accomplished and educated in law and Slavic languages, and continuing studies in psychology. Etty is rooming with a group of friends and has another very influential group surrounding her therapist/teacher in psychology. He is Julius Spier, a Jewish immigrant from Germany. Trained by Carl Jung and a self-taught reader of palms, he founded the field of psychochirology, the study of hands.

More than twice her age, Julius Spier became her lover as well as teacher. He seemed to have the practice of fostering deep emotional and physical attachments with his disciples. His relationship with Etty created inner conflict for her. "I am accomplished in bed… and love does suit me to perfection, and yet it remains a mere trifle, set apart from what is truly essential, and deep inside me something is still locked away."[1] Etty's apparent freedom in all things sexual leaves her uncertain and unhappy. "I seem to be a match for most of life's problems, and yet deep down something like a tightly-wound ball of twine binds me relentlessly and at times I am nothing more or less than a miserable, frightened creature, despite the clarity with which I can express myself."[2]

The substance of these few words is repeated over and over in Etty's journal with a variation on the theme. Etty goes through the age-long struggle of not wanting to be under the domination of S. (as she refers to Spier in her diary) and giving into his physical demands. She wants to be part of this intellectual group surrounding him without becoming dependent upon him. Her words are inconsistent with her actions. One day Etty goes to a lecture by S. and sees all the young girls clearly attracted to him, even some Aryan ones. This caused unease in Etty. She watched S. speak to a young Aryan girl who gave him "a smile so charged with devotion that it almost hurt me. I was suddenly filled with a vague sense of unease… had the feeling: that man is stealing this young girl's smile, and all the tenderness this child bears him is stolen from someone else, from the man who will later be her own. What he did was pretty mean and unfair. He was clearly a dangerous man."[3]

The words appear to be insightful, but Etty's emotions and own insecurity are far from the

Confusion

words. For many months Etty continues in the same relationship with S. and his group of devotees. As a result, inner peace eludes her. Self-knowledge is a hard reality and rarely a straight path. She keeps at the struggle and admits, "I am really a very serious person who does not like to make light of love… all the adventures and transient relationships I have had have made me utterly miserable, tearing me apart."[4] Etty the intellectual turns to the poetry of Rilke, the novels of Tolstoy, her philosophy, and her psychology books. Etty, the emotional young woman, continues her relationship with S. and with others as well.

Ironically, it was the encroaching menace of the Nazi reign of terror inflicted on the people of Holland that freed Etty from the unhealthy and strangling hold that S. had on her. "More arrests, more terror, concentration camps, the arbitrary dragging off of fathers, sisters, brothers. We seek the meaning of life, wondering whether any meaning can be left. But that is something each one of us must settle with himself and with God."[5] Life had become so fierce that all but the essentials fell away from Etty. Sorrow and fear have a way of winnowing out false premises and lame excuses.

Nothing happens quickly. For every new insight Etty gleans, there are days and weeks of friendships and lovers, clarity and darkness, hope and despair. Etty has felt the first conscious stirrings of God within her being, and she has the sense that this God is not meant to be an escape from life but a presence in it. "There is a really deep well inside me. And in it dwells God. Sometimes I am there too. But more often stones and grit block the well, and God is buried beneath."[6] It is the beginning for Etty; she is on the journey now with her distant yet immanent God. Instinctively she knows that God will not be found outside the reality of her life. Her search for God is also a search with God. It will begin from her own reality with all its agony.

"I want to know this century of ours inside and out. I feel it every day anew. I run my fingertips along the contours of our age."[7] And within this headstrong, independent young woman comes an openness to God that is courageous and brave. "I sometimes feel I am in some blazing purgatory and that I am being forged into something else. But into what? I can only be passive, allow it to happen to me."[8] A seismic shift has occurred within Etty in six months. If her journey for meaning in life had been to this point a whirlwind of activity engaging all her faculties and body, it will be as nothing compared to what awaits Etty now that she has shifted her attention to God.

KNEELING

Not having been raised in a religious family, God and prayer were new to Etty. She was young and ambitiously intellectual. What couldn't be rationalized and explained seemed unreal, until God began a journey into Etty. Before she could be precise with her words or her feelings, she had a sense of God. "God, you are with me after all, if only a little bit."[9] After experiencing the insistent stirrings of a call from God, Etty began attending to it and realized that she was always with God and God was with her. Simultaneously she was searching and finding, being sought and being found.

Etty yearned to respond and she was intrigued by kneeling before God. The physical act seemed to be an enormous step into a relationship with an unknown yet fully present God. Etty called herself "the girl who could not kneel." It seems difficult to fathom the enormity of the physical act of kneeling before God. For Etty, it embodied her surrender to a new way of living, to an unknown entity she called God. It was far more than bending her knees. It was an act of massive consequence for Etty even though she couldn't express why it was so.

Etty must have talked about this with some of her friends, because she remarks about Tide, one of her roommates, as a strong woman who knelt down in the middle of her room to ask God for help whenever she was in trouble. Etty found Tide's gestures "mature and certain."[10] So Etty began to try out kneeling for herself. She practiced in the bathroom first and then in her own room. She prayed, "O, Lord, let me feel at one with myself. Let me perform a thousand daily tasks with love, but let every one spring from a greater central core of devotion and love."[11]

An incident of being seen by one of her lovers in the act of kneeling reveals Etty's insecurity about what she was doing. "This morning, in the gray dawn, in a fit of nervous agitation, I suddenly found myself on the floor between Hans' stripped bed and his typewriter, huddled up, my head on the ground. As if I were trying to seize peace by force. And when Hans came in and seemed a bit taken aback by the spectacle, I told him I was looking for a button. But that was a lie."[12]

Kneeling eventually became a gesture of love. It became spontaneous and moved beyond the em-

Kneeling

barrassment stage in Etty's life. "Last night, shortly before going to bed, I suddenly went down on my knees in the middle of this large room, between the steel chairs and the matting. Almost automatically. Forced to the ground by something stronger than myself. Some time ago I said to myself, 'I am a kneeler in training.' I was still embarrassed by this act, as intimate as gestures of love that cannot be put into words either, except by a poet."[13]

Etty herself acknowledges her kneeling is not an end in itself but a beginning. "But now I sometimes actually drop to my knees beside my bed even on a cold winter night. And I listen to myself allow myself to be led, not by anything on the outside but by what wells up from within. It's still no more than a beginning… but it has taken root."[14]

Etty's diary entry of late November, nearly nine months after beginning the diary, records a break-through experience. She is riding her bicycle through a cold dark street at night and she finds herself conversing with God. She finds herself surrendering to God. "God, take me by the hand, I shall follow You dutifully, and not resist too much. I shall evade none of the tempests life has in store for me.… I shall follow wherever Your hand leads me and shall try not to be afraid. I shall try to spread some of my warmth, of my genuine love for others, wherever I go."[15] During this same experience of prayer, Etty realizes that she is free of S. and admits that she imagined that she was free all along. This is the start of a pattern in Etty's life. As she advances in prayer and relationship with God, that inner calm and freedom that had been a burning desire of Etty's, develops and grows. Etty is growing up emotionally as well as spiritually. She becomes free to pray and to kneel whenever she desires. She becomes free of her dependence upon sexual encounters as a way of relating and discovering life. Life is far richer than Etty ever imagined or conceived, beyond her intellectual prowess and insatiable appetite for the approval of her friends.

DAILY LIFE

Etty's newly embarked-upon journey with God first took her to her knees but then moved her into the daily reality of life under the German occupation of Holland. Etty, as a member of the Jewish Council, had to meet with the Gestapo on a regular basis. The illusion of their working together for the good of the Jews was widespread. The Jewish Council initially thought they could negotiate in certain areas of German policy. It was all a giant scam to control the Jewish people in Holland until they could be shipped to the concentration camps.

The bizarre and the human blended into the rhythms of daily life. Etty writes of an encounter at Gestapo headquarters which reveals both sides of humanity. The Jewish Council had been summoned to answer questions concerning their finances. While waiting in line with S. to report to the Gestapo, a former client of S.'s recognizes him, has a conversation and then fills out all the forms for them so they no longer have to wait in that line. A few days later, Etty was back in the same hall, again summoned by the Gestapo. This time another young man was moving among the Jewish people, yelling at them and harassing them. Etty was not intimidated by him, which, of course, irritated the officer to no end. He made a special effort to frighten Etty, but he couldn't. Etty said she was not frightened because she saw clearly his own weaknesses and fears. Etty was realistic and she explains her perception of him, "I know that pitiful young men like that are dangerous as soon as they are let loose on mankind. But all the blame must be put on the system that uses such people. What needs eradicating is the evil in man. Not man himself."[16]

Etty goes further in her reflections on the experience of evil. "Something else about this morning: the perception, very strongly borne in, that despite all the suffering and injustice I cannot hate others."[17] Then she continues with her day. In the midst of the trauma, Etty writes about enjoying a drink of Van Houten's cocoa, a cup of coffee, cheap cigarettes and meeting an old boyfriend in the street one night. As they reminisce about their youth and speak of his coming marriage, they both feel the impending doom. "There are few illusions left to us. Life is going to be very hard. We shall

Daily Life

be torn apart, all who are dear to one another. I don't think the time is very far off now. We shall have to steel ourselves inwardly more and more."[18] They depart from each other not knowing if they will ever meet again or even if they can write to each other.

The rules have become very restrictive as to where Jews can walk. They can no longer walk along the Promenade or in any wood and "every miserable little clump of two or three trees has been pronounced a wood with a board nailed up. No admittance to Jews."[19] However, even the Gestapo cannot stop the breezes from reaching Etty. "I suddenly felt the caress of balmy spring air. Yes, I thought, that's how it should be. Why shouldn't one feel an immense, tender ecstasy of love for the spring, or for all humanity."[20]

Etty and her friends continue, celebrating the daily successes of obtaining a sack of coal, some wood, sugar and biscuits, tea and cake. They still play music, the musicians still practice. Turnips are bartered for sauerkraut. A walk at night with a friend is treasured. A gift of a few eggs is cause for celebration. In the midst of all this suffocation of freedom and fear, Etty admits, "I suddenly have the urge to kneel down in some quiet corner."[21] Or after relating the mundane details of a day, she inserts, "And sometimes the most important thing in a whole day is the rest we take between two deep breaths, or the turning inwards in prayer for five short minutes."[22]

At the risk of portraying herself as fully calm and peaceful through all the tragedies of the days of increased restrictions for the Jews and significant numbers of them being moved to concentration camps, Etty writes of her times of hopelessness and feelings of futility in the face of the agony. With Etty it is always personal. She speaks of one mother, Ilse Blumenthal, who has lost her sons to the camps. She worries about one lesbian woman who is struggling with self-acceptance. She acknowledges the hunger crisis by writing about the adventure of bacon and eggs. She mourns the destruction of cities, of her Rotterdam.

Always Etty, like the psalmist centuries earlier, ends with her God. "Monday night, on going to bed, I said, 'Dear God, today I cannot praise you; I honestly don't feel happy enough.'"[23] Etty's very honest prayer signifies the depth of her growing relationship with her God. There is no place in her life with others or with God for superficial pretense. Life demands too much at times such as hers. She cannot waste a single moment, a single day, a single prayer. Each cup of coffee may be the last; each entry in her diary the final one. The details of Etty's days have become filled with gracious tenderness,

Daily Life

to be savored in love not wasted in hatred. She clearly has chosen the way to respond to each day, regardless of the actions of others.

Engaged profoundly in her times, Etty enters each day with God, her newfound lover. "It (kneeling) has become a gesture embedded in my body, needing to be expressed from time to time. And I remember: 'The girl who could not kneel,' and the rough coconut matting in the bathroom. When I write these things down, I still feel a little ashamed, as if I were writing about the most intimate of intimate matters. Much more bashful than if I had to write about my love-life. But is there anything as intimate as man's relationship to God?"[24]

SUFFERING

Six centuries before the birth of Jesus, twenty-six centuries before World War II, a man of peace lived in Judah. His name was Jeremiah. His entire life was lived in a tumultuous time. As God's prophet, he was called to denounce violence and teach worship of a God of love. Not an easy task. Suffering was his lot in life. There is no way of knowing how familiar Etty Hillesum was with the Book of Jeremiah in the Bible. Etty writes nothing about her religious formation as a Jew, if she had any. Whether she knew Jeremiah or not, her own path through suffering mirrors his in significant ways.

Etty was not a prophet in the biblical sense of a leader called by God to instruct the people in the ways of God. However, she was one in the sense of a person who responds in faith to the realities around her. As Jeremiah's world was crashing around him from war and oppression, ending with exile in Babylon, so Etty's world is filled with war and oppression, ending with exile to the camps. Jeremiah and Etty had to face unbearable suffering which would eventually destroy many of their people.

In times such as these, many lose faith and refuse to worship a God who could allow such things to happen. Everyone has a breaking point and unmitigated suffering can lead to it. From the beginning Etty never blames God; she sees the evil around her as the work of human persons. "All the appalling things that happen are no mysterious threats from afar, but arise from fellow beings very close to us."[25]

Etty seems to possess a pragmatism that takes her past her emotions into a clear view of people. In his agony, Jeremiah cried out that he must bear the grief of his time. Etty says, "And you must be able to bear your sorrow; even if it seems to crush you, you will be able to stand up again, for human beings are so strong, and your sorrow must become an integral part of yourself, part of your body and soul, you mustn't run away from it, but bear it like an adult."[26] Where did she get the strength to write such words? Sixty years later, three generations removed from the holocaust, it is still impossible to take in the degree of suffering inflicted upon the

Suffering

Jewish people by the Nazi war machine.

This is far more than maintaining a positive attitude; it is raw faith in the goodness of God and of other people. It is a profound sense of humanity at its best and at its worst. It is the courage to bear the suffering life holds. It is critical to remember as we reflect on Etty's stance toward suffering that she was also doing everything she could to alleviate it. Masochism is not an admirable virtue and there was none of that in Etty.

Critical to understanding Etty's ability to endure suffering is her refusal to hate. "Give your sorrow all the space and shelter in yourself that is its due… if you do not clear a decent shelter for your sorrow, and instead reserve most of the space inside you for hatred and thoughts of revenge – from which new sorrows will be born for others – then sorrow will never cease in this world and it will multiply."[27] This lesson has been reiterated throughout history by some who have suffered greatly. A South African woman, whose husband and son were brutally tortured and murdered during apartheid, publicly forgave the man who did it because she did not want to hate in memory of her family. An American woman whose son was murdered forgave his murderer because she said she had a limited amount of energy. If she chose to expend it on hate, there would be nothing left for love.

Certainly for those who read and believe the Christian scriptures, there is Jesus who taught love of enemies and died forgiving those who crucified him. We know Etty was familiar with that because she says, "There is the Gospel of St. Matthew morning and night, and now and then a few words on this paper."[28] It is possible not to be a Christian and to still be moved by the life of Jesus. Mohandas Gandhi is the perfect example of this – a faithful Hindu who based his teachings on the Sermon on the Mount from St. Matthew's Gospel.

Whatever her source for inspiration, Etty was actively employed in treating her oppressors as human persons not as enemies. She prayed repeatedly to have the courage to love. "This morning, early, I knelt down in the living room among all the bread crumbs on the carpet. And if I should have to say aloud what I said in my prayers, it would go something like this: 'Oh, Lord, this day, this day – it seems so heavy to me, let me bear it well to its end... my strength to bear it is not so great.... But Lord, help me not to waste a drop of my energy on fear and anxiety, but grant me all the resilience I need to bear this day.' German soldiers were already drilling at the Skating Club. And so I prayed, 'God, do not let me dissipate my strength,

Suffering

not the least little bit of strength, on useless hatred against these soldiers. Let me save my strength for better things.'"[29]

Etty has to find in her situation what Jeremiah had to find in his – a path of honesty with oneself, others and God. For Etty, the woman who loved to love, it is not surprising that the language of bodily love becomes the language of her love for others, even the Germans. "One hand is all we need to caress. And a little work. And our work can be done anywhere, wherever there is a human being, be he only a camp guard."[30]

PRAYER

Once Etty's strong will teaches her equally strong legs to bend, once she learns to kneel, prayer becomes as essential as breathing. Prayer becomes her strength, her refuge, her joy, her hope, her teacher and her lover. "The threat grows ever greater, and terror increases from day to day. I draw prayer around me like a dark protective wall; withdraw inside it as one might into a convent cell and then step outside again, calmer and stronger and more collected again. I can imagine times to come when I shall stay on my knees for days on end waiting until the protective walls are strong enough to prevent my going to pieces altogether, my being lost and utterly devastated."[32]

Hiding is not Etty's response. She faces life as it is. Her God is deeply involved in her time; eternal truths are not separate from the reality of the world. Day by day the march of war and hatred fill Etty's life and dog her steps. More restrictions are being promulgated; more people are being taken away. Etty stays with her people and with her God. She is at home with both and responsible for both. Without rabbi or pastor, Etty is learning faith and prayer.

The Spirit of God has become her teacher and mentor, guiding her through the anti-Semitism and flames of World War II; just as God led the people of Israel through the desert for forty years with a cloud by day and a fire by night. As they were fed their daily portion of manna, so is God feeding Etty her daily portion of strength and courage.

Etty needs God and God needs Etty – a simple statement, yet one that eludes many. It is not sufficient to be drawn to deep prayer or to seek times and places for contemplation. The movement to God of necessity includes the movement to others. Etty is becoming totally immersed in prayer, in God and in the suffering of others. Prayer is no escape; on the contrary it is a most courageous act, especially in the face of daily terror.

To awake day after day to greet the God of life in faith, hope and love is a courageous human endeavor, demanding perseverance and a resiliency stronger than any tragedy that can mar fragile humanity. The poet John Berryman speaks of such courage when writing about Anne Frank: "She was forced to mature, in order to survive; the hardest

Prayer

challenge, let's say, that a person can face without defeat is the best for him."[32]

To persevere in prayer when all is falling apart around you is humanity at its best. The mystic (a person who consciously lives in God) is not one who runs from the realities of life but one who embraces them. After describing the overcrowded living conditions in the Jewish quarter, eight people to a room, Etty reports, "And now Jews may no longer visit the greengrocers' shops, they will soon have to hand in their bicycles, they may no longer travel by tram and they must be off the streets by 8 o'clock at night."[33] Etty perseveres, "…the most ominous measures… have no power against my inner certainty and confidence."[34]

Etty is clear about prayer and its rootedness in reality. "Mysticism must rest on crystal-clear honesty, can only come after things have been stripped down to their naked reality."[35] How courageous to dare to live with "crystal-clear honesty." No one enjoys the vulnerability of sheer naked reality. It is easier to try to escape into drugs, alcohol, work, religion, pleasure-seeking or the thousands of other ways to avoid facing one's true self.

The journey to human maturity demands great honesty and courage. If it is to be undertaken, often an outside event sparks the inner search. It can be illness, loss of a loved one, unemployment, love, war, a tragic accident, crime, infidelity, death or birth, or any of the myriad realities that come into a single individual's life. The horror of the Holocaust was Etty's turning point. It is easy to understand why one could lose their faith or their mind during the horror of it.

A Holocaust survivor, Viktor Frankl endured the torture and taught the world that having meaning in life had a great deal to do with surviving prolonged terror. Love became Etty's meaning in life – not the love of just one person, but the love of all people in God. The mystic embraces all in one, with the ability to find beauty. Anne Frank, the teenager who was experiencing the same fears as Etty and Viktor Frankl, cried aloud that she believed in the goodness of people. Edith Stein, another holocaust victim, brushed and combed the children's hair in the concentration camp, while knowing that they were marked for death.

The miracle of life in the face of death is indeed a profound sign of God's presence. We know Etty prayed always and we know she possessed profound faith and unshakable hope; we can assume the connection. "They can harass us, they can rob us of our material goods, of our freedom of movement, but we ourselves forfeit our greatest assets by our misguided compliance. By our feelings of being persecuted, humiliated and oppressed. By

Prayer

our own hatred. By our swagger which hides our fear. We may of course be sad and depressed by what has been done to us; that is only human and understandable. However, our greatest injury is one we inflict upon ourselves. I find life beautiful and I feel free. The sky within me is as wide as the one stretching above my head. I believe in God and I believe in man… I am a happy person and I hold life dear indeed, in this year of Our Lord 1942, the umpteenth year of the war."[36]

JASMINE

The worse the situation gets, the more confident Etty becomes. Word is out that hundreds of thousands of Jews have perished in the concentration camps in Poland. Etty is separated from her family, but still knows where they are, and yet admits that soon she probably won't. She faces the prospect of her own death. There is no escaping the trauma. "Even if we stay alive we shall carry the wounds with us throughout our lives. And yet I don't think life is meaningless. And God is not accountable to us for the senseless harm we cause one another. We are accountable to him! I have already died a thousand deaths in a thousand concentration camps. I know about everything and am no longer appalled by the latest reports. In one way or another I know it all. And yet I find life beautiful and meaningful. From minute to minute."[37]

One aspect of Etty's poetic nature was her appreciation of nature – the color and vastness of the sky, the smell of spring, the hunger of winter, the wide trunk of a tree. "There was a riot of bird song on the flat, graveled roof, and a pigeon outside my wide open window. And the early morning sun."[38] No image is more frequently used in her diary than the jasmine flower. As lovers have favorite songs or places of special memories, Etty met her God often over jasmine. Beauty touched her and her soul soared above the mire of anti-Semitism and all its ugly consequences.

"Sun on the balcony and a light breeze through the jasmine… I shall linger another ten minutes with the jasmine…. How exotic the jasmine looks, so delicate and dazzling against the mud-brown walls. I cannot take in how beautiful this jasmine is. But there is no need to. It is enough simply to believe in miracles in the twentieth century. And I do, even though the lice will be eating me up in Poland before long."[39]

Reality has become deadly serious. There is no way out for Etty and for the 155,000 Jews in Holland. Her words describing the day-to-day existence are clearly fraught with possible extermination. Etty holds pain and beauty in one courageous heart. Jasmine, death, and God become inextricably bound, the source of union being love.

"And don't we live an entire life each one of

our days, and does it really matter if we live a few days more or less? I am in Poland every day, on the battlefields, if that's what one can call them. I often see visions of poisonous green smoke. I am with the hungry, with the ill-treated and the dying, every day, but I am also with the jasmine and with that piece of sky beyond my window; there is room for everything in a single life. For belief in God and for a miserable end."[40]

Etty looked at the face of persecution without denial of its reality in her situation. "I want to feel with my fingertips the contours of the times."[41] Still Etty felt beauty touch her. For many, these were times of naked vulnerability. People acted differently knowing they could meet death at any moment. "Between our eyes and hands, and mouths there now flows a constant stream of tenderness, a stream in which all petty desires seem to have been extinguished. All that matters now is to be kind to each other with all the goodness that is in us. And every encounter is also a farewell."[42]

Etty's mysticism was for others. "All the strength and love and faith in God which one possesses, and which have grown so miraculously in me of late, must be there for everyone who chances to cross one's path… out of my love for him (God) I must draw strength and love for everyone who needs it."[43]

As Etty's soul savored the jasmine given her by her lover God, she returned the love to all she met. "The jasmine behind my house has been completely ruined by the rains and storms of the last few days, its white blossoms are floating about in muddy black pools on the low garage roof. But somewhere inside me the jasmine continues to blossom undisturbed, just as profusely and delicately as ever it did. And it spreads its scent round the House in which you dwell, oh God. You can see I look after you, I bring you not only my tears and my forebodings on this stormy, gray Sunday morning, I even bring you scented jasmine. And I shall bring you all the flowers I shall meet on the way, and truly there are many of those. I shall try to make you at home always. Even if I should be locked up in a narrow cell and a cloud should drift past my small barred window, then I shall bring you that cloud, oh God."[44]

When the beautiful flowers have been knocked down by the storms, Etty herself becomes the loveliest of jasmine flowers before God and her people. Together they become the fragrant flowers the storm cannot destroy.

FAITH

In addition to all the reflections Etty made about life and love, resistance and compliance, danger and hope, she also consciously thought of her own faith journey. She was aware of the great spiritual journey she was taking. "There are moments when I can see right through life and the human heart and… am filled with a faith in God which has grown so quickly inside me that it frightened me at first but has now become inseparable from me."[45]

Clearly Etty acknowledges her faith as gift. It seems not to be tied to any specific practice of religion in synagogue or church. The times in which she was living prevented many external practices, since the ability to move about was so restricted. Etty speaks throughout the diary of her mentors and inspirations in faith: the poetry of Rainer Maria Rilke, the novels of Dostoevsky and Tolstoy, the art of Michelangelo and Leonardo, the writings of St. Augustine and the Gospel of St. Matthew. Her sources of inspiration were eclectic, coming through philosophy and poetry, art and literature. Etty fed on the psalms daily. "Those psalms which have become part of my daily life were excellent fare on an empty stomach."[46]

It is clear by her diary entries that Etty invested time into her newly discovered faith in God. She prayed and contemplated God and read the book of her life with God. The effect of faith or the fruit of faith was fourfold: it gave Etty a sense of protection, increased her self-confidence, made her happy, and brought her to the experience of self-sacrifice for others.

Faith kept Etty safe inside no matter what was done to her by the Germans. "Many accuse me of indifference and passivity when I refuse to go into hiding; they say that I have given up. They say everyone must try to stay out of their clutches…. And the funny thing is I don't feel I'm in their clutches anyway, whether I stay or am sent away.… I don't feel in anybody's clutches; I feel safe in God's arms… and no matter whether I am sitting at this beloved old desk now, or in a bare room in the Jewish district or perhaps in a labor camp under SS guards in a month's time – I shall always feel safe in God's arms.… I may face cruelty and depravation the likes of which I cannot imagine in even my

Faith

wildest fantasies. Yet all this is as nothing to the immeasurable expanse of my faith in God and my inner receptiveness."[47]

Faith gave Etty a resiliency and a drive that were conversely proportional to the external restrictions enforced by the Nazi soldiers. The highly-emotional, insecure young woman is replaced by a fiercely confident and outspoken one. She is no longer under the spell of her friends and lovers or even of the Germans. Her faith itself is a confident one. She converses with God rather than pleads. She and God are in a profound partnership, yet Etty knows who is God and who is not. "I shall never burden my today with cares about my tomorrow although that takes some practice. Each day is sufficient unto itself. I shall try to help You, God, to stop my strength ebbing away, though I cannot vouch for that in advance. But one thing is becoming increasingly clear to me: that You cannot help us, that we must help You to help ourselves... and defend Your dwelling place inside us to the last."[48] These words of Etty's are complex and reflect a mature relationship with God. God is not a being above us who is expected to solve all problems and intervene in evil realities to protect the innocent. Etty's God is friend not fixer. Her prayers are conversations not pleas. God is present with Etty not distant from her. "I am beginning to feel a little more peaceful, God, thanks to this conversation with You. You are sure to go through lean times with me now and then, when my faith weakens a little, but believe me, I shall always labor for You and remain faithful to You and I shall never drive You from my presence."[49]

It is hard to imagine the need for self-sacrifice in the midst of the ravages of war and the intended annihilation of the Jews by Hitler's design and master plan. To survive what someone had no choice about seemed to be more than enough effort, yet there were many who thought of others and acted heroically. Maximilian Kolbe, a Catholic priest, took the place of a father of a family and was executed as punishment for an escape by another prisoner. Dietrich Bonhoeffer, a Lutheran theologian, returned to Germany after escaping to America, so he could suffer the same fate as his people. Etty went to the camp at Westerbork earlier than she had to so as to spare someone else from going. "I don't think I would feel happy if I were exempted from what so many others have to suffer. They keep telling me that someone like me has a duty to go into hiding, because I have so many things to do in life, so much to give. But I know that whatever I may have to give to others, I can give it no matter where I am, here in the circle of my friends or over there, in a concentration camp.

Faith

And it is sheer arrogance to think oneself too good to share the fate of the masses."⁵⁰

The incredible humility of the woman! To think herself at one with others, that no one is more significant or worthy than any other. She was in total contrast with the society around her which was proclaiming by torture, extermination and war that some persons are more important than others. The conversion has been remarkable. Etty, the young woman of obsessive introspection and worry about herself, has become Etty, the self-effacing woman for others.

With this dramatic change comes fearlessness, peace and happiness. Etty could face Hitler himself without experiencing intimidation. "I am not afraid of them (Germans) either, I don't know why. I am so calm…. This bit of history we are experiencing right now is something I know I can stand up to… but sometimes I feel as if a layer of ashes were being sprinkled over my heart, as if my face were withering and decaying before my very eyes… but then everything falls back into place. For once you have begun to walk with God, you need only keep on walking with Him and all of life becomes one long stroll – such a marvelous feeling."⁵¹

Etty's calm fearlessness did not exclude times of despair and imminent fear, but these moments did not rule her thoughts and actions. "It is good to have moments of despair and of temporary extinction; continuous calm would be superhuman. But now I know again that I shall always get the better of despair."[52] God did not desert Etty at her low times; neither did Etty deny God in those moments. "There will always be a small patch of sky above, and there will always be enough space to fold two hands in prayer."[53] Etty's love became a flame of happiness that could not be extinguished.

TRANSFORMATION

*W*hen faced with mortal anguish, some succumb to despair, some to panic, others to survival for its own sake, and the rare few surrender in total abandonment to love so strong that transformation of the very reality which caused the pain in the first place can happen. Etty was one of the few. As her life became more tenuous and entered into its final months, she cut through the searing terror with the steel strong blade of compassion and forgiveness. She became a person of transformation of herself and of the whole world.

Utter selflessness is the mark of a person of transformation, surrender to God is its path, and love is its fruit. Etty evolved into a person for others. Life was becoming a hell all around her. At one point she mentioned that Dante's *Inferno* would be "comic relief" compared to life for the Jews at this time in history. The peacefulness of Etty's own inner being allowed her the space and energy to care for others and to worry about their lack of inner preparation for the struggles awaiting them.

"When I pray, I never pray for myself, always for others."[54] Etty's prayers were always for strength to bear the burdens of the day; she did not abandon hope in the midst of the fray.

Etty's work load shifted in the summer before her own deportation. Work in the Cultural Affairs Department of the Jewish Council put her in the heart of the chaos. It wore her out physically and emotionally, but it did not rob her of her inner resources. She continued to care for people as she was able. She refused to give up hope. Her own faith gave her enough strength to be a person of "bright and bubbling good humor." Etty brought her red and white roses into the gloom of others' lives. When they asked her how she could think of flowers in such times, Etty's response was, "They are as real as all the misery I witness each day."[55]

Things were happening so fast; life was going at breakneck speed and Etty's inner life was keeping the same pace… too fast for words. "Indeed I shall have to invent an entirely new language to express everything that has moved my heart these last few days."[56] "To think that one small human heart can experience so much, of God, so much suffering and so much love, I am grateful to You, God, for having chosen my heart, in these times,

Transformation

to experience all the things it has experienced."[57]

Etty absorbed her days' happenings into her heart which rested in God's heart, and she brought all her people with her. She knew she was being transformed. "I believe I have gradually managed to attain the simplicity for which I have always longed."[58] She knew she was precious to God and necessary in God's work. "I have often felt and still feel like a ship with a precious cargo; the moorings have been slipped and now the ship is free to take its load to any place in earth."[59] "I feel as if I were the guardian of a precious slice of life, with all the responsibility that entails."[60]

Etty's soul had been formed and reformed, "A soul is forged out of fire and rock crystal. Something rigorous, hard in an Old Testament sense, but also as gentle as the gesture with which his tender fingertips sometimes stroked my eyelashes."[61] She had learned to take her wildly spontaneous thirst for life and love and use it for God and for others. "Why not turn that love, which cannot be bestowed on another… into a force that benefits the whole community and that might still be love? And if we attempt that transformation, are we not standing on the solid ground of the real world, of reality?"[62]

As broken-hearted and hungry people lined up for registration for the camps, Etty moved among them, often wordlessly, holding them, looking at them with love, comforting by her presence, strengthening by her own courage, smiling for the "huddled, shattered scraps of humanity." "I am not afraid to look suffering straight in the eyes. And at the end of each day, there was always the feeling: I love people so much."[63]

"Sometimes it (Etty's soul) bursts into full flame within me…. I rejoice and exult time and again, 'Oh God: I am grateful to You for having given me this life'"[64] Etty speaks constantly to God in her final diary entries. She has become one with God; she has been transformed in God. "Alone for once in the middle of the night, God and I have been left together, and I feel all the richer and at peace for it."[65]

Her life's journey almost at an end, Etty goes back in gratitude to repeat her mantra of conversion: "When the turmoil becomes too great and I am completely at my wit's end, then I still have my folded hands and bended knee…. What a strange story it really is, my story: the girl who could not kneel. Or its variation: the girl who learned to pray. That is my most intimate gesture, more intimate even than being with a man."[66]

Etty went far beyond prayer with words; she prayed with her entire life. "I have broken my body like bread and shared it out among men. And why

Transformation

not; they were hungry and had gone without for so long."[67]

Etty became food and solace for Germans and Jews alike. The final words of Etty's diary sum up her faith: "We should be willing to act as a balm for all wounds."[68]

FINAL THOUGHTS

Westerbork, which was in the eastern part of the Netherlands, was not one of the main concentration camps. It was a transit camp for Jews before being sent to the camps in Poland or Germany. Most went to Auschwitz from Westerbork. Etty spent over a year there but in the first months she made some trips back to Amsterdam on "business" for the Jewish Council. She used those trips to write the final section of her diary, to convey messages, and to procure medicine. Once she was no longer allowed to leave, Etty sent letters. A handful of them survived the war.

All the horror that Etty anticipated was happening in Westerbork: unbearable misery, hunger, overcrowding, illness. "People living like so many rats in a sewer... many dying children... thin waxen faces... registration, more registration, frisking by half-grown NSB men (Dutch Nazis), quarantine, a foretaste of martyrdom lasting hours and hours."[69]

In the same letter, Etty continues, "The misery here is quite terrible and yet, late at night when the day has slunk away into the depths behind me, I often walk with a spring in my step along the barbed wire and then time and again it soars straight from my heart… that feeling that life is glorious and magnificent, and that one day we shall be building a whole new world. Against every new outrage and every fresh horror we shall put up one more piece of love and goodness, drawing strength from within ourselves. We may suffer but we must not succumb."[70]

The letters describe the daily struggle for food and rest, for hope and companionship. Etty's brother Mischa and her parents are in Westerbork with her and her heart breaks for them. She worries about their health, their stamina. And Etty sees mothers having babies, knowing they will be the first to be sent to the camps for extermination. Etty realizes that the same concern and love she has for her family she also has for others. "I told myself it must be wrong to be so overcome with grief and concern for one's family that one has little thought and love left over for one's neighbor. I see more and more that love for all our neighbors, for everyone made in God's image, must take pride of place over love for one's nearest and dearest."[71]

A smattering of stories portrays the insanity

Final Thoughts

of Westerbork. A nine month-old baby is in the prison barracks because she had a criminal record – she was abandoned. A three year-old broke a window and was afraid of being sent to the prison. A small boy runs from the transport train. He is captured, but fifty other children are sent along as punishment for his actions. And the many deaths due to suicide, disease, starvation, deprivation – Etty writes of all of them. She is spared nothing. She endures. "I always end up with just one single word: God.... And all my creative powers are translated into inner dialogues with You; the beat of my heart has grown deeper, more active and yet more peaceful, and it is as if I were all the time storing up inner riches."[72]

> "We suffer, we suffer into truth.
>   In our sleep pain that cannot forget falls
>   drop by drop
>   Upon the human heart and in our despair,
>   against our will,
>   Comes wisdom through the awful grace
>   of God."[73]

Sent off in wagons to trains, some will die along the way. The train cars are packed with people, bags and one bucket for their needs. The commandants parade the length of the train and then order the doors slammed shut, cutting off air and light for the three days journey to Auschwitz. A thousand people per train. "One more piece of our camp has been amputated. Next week another piece will follow. This is what has been happening now for over a year, week in and week out. We are left with just a few thousand… we are all marked down to share that fate; of that I have not a moment's doubt."[74]

Etty, her parents and her brother Mischa were sent on transport to Auschwitz on September 7, 1943. Etty died there on November 30, 1943. Her last written words are from a postcard which she threw from the transport train on the way to her death. Farmers found it and mailed it. On it Etty wrote, "We have left the camp singing."[75] A grateful heart died a heroic death and left us a legacy for hope in all times and all circumstances.

"You have made me so rich, oh God, please let me share out Your beauty with open hands. My life has become one great dialogue. Sometimes when I stand in some corner of the camp, my feet planted on Your earth, my eyes raised towards Your Heaven, tears sometimes run down my face, tears of deep emotion and gratitude. At night, too, when I lie in my bed and rest in You, oh God, tears of gratitude run down my face, and that is my prayer."[76]

Footnotes

Introduction
1. Etty Hillesum, *An Interrupted Life: The Diaries of Etty Hillesum, 1941-1943* (New York: Washington Square Press, 1985) 62.
2. Ibid.

Text
1. Ibid. 1.
2. Ibid. 2.
3. Ibid. 4.
4. Ibid. 16.
5. Ibid. 28.
6. Ibid. 44.
7. Ibid. 44.
8. Ibid. 44,45.
9. Ibid. 52.
10. Ibid. 79.
11. Ibid. 71.
12. Ibid. 79.
13. Ibid. 76.
14. Ibid. 81.
15. Ibid. 64.
16. Ibid. 89.
17. Ibid. 89.
18. Ibid. 91.
19. Ibid. 93.
20. Ibid. 92.
21. Ibid. 94.
22. Ibid. 96.
23. Ibid. 104.
24. Ibid. 110.
25. Ibid. 89.
26. Ibid. 100.
27. Ibid. 100.
28. Ibid. 115.
29. Ibid. 113, 114.
30. Ibid. 133.
31. Ibid. 139.
32. John Berryman, "The Development of Anne Frank," *The Freedom of the Poet* (New York: Farrar, Straus & Giroux, 1976) 104.
33. *An Interrupted Life*, 146.
34. Ibid. 146.

[35] Ibid. 149.
[36] Ibid. 151.
[37] Ibid. 157.
[38] Ibid. 169.
[39] Ibid. 158, 159.
[40] Ibid. 159.
[41] Ibid. 219.
[42] Ibid. 172.
[43] Ibid. 175.
[44] Ibid. 188.
[45] Ibid. 179.
[46] Ibid. 170.
[47] Ibid. 184, 185.
[48] Ibid. 186, 187.
[49] Ibid. 187.
[50] Ibid. 185.
[51] Ibid. 189.
[52] Ibid. 191.
[53] Ibid. 190.
[54] Ibid. 192.
[55] Ibid. 197.
[56] Ibid. 194.
[57] Ibid. 207.
[58] Ibid. 196.
[59] Ibid. 218.
[60] Ibid. 195.
[61] Ibid. 241.
[62] Ibid. 218.
[63] Ibid. 238.
[64] Ibid. 241.
[65] Ibid. 237.
[66] Ibid. 240.
[67] Ibid. 242.
[68] Ibid. 243.
[69] Ibid. 246.
[70] Ibid. 247.
[71] Ibid. 251.
[72] Ibid. 255.
[73] Aeschylus, *Agamemmon,* trans. Edith Hamilton (New York: W.W. Norton & Co., 1937) #179-84.
[74] *An Interrupted Life* 272.
[75] Ibid. xvi.
[76] Ibid. 255.

\ULS

This book was produced by ST PAULS/Alba House, the Society of St. Paul, an international religious congregation of priests and brothers dedicated to serving the Church through the communications media.

For information regarding this and associated ministries of the Pauline Family of Congregations, write to the Vocation Director, Society of St. Paul, 2187 Victory Blvd., Staten Island, New York 10314-6603. Phone (718) 982-5709; or E-mail: vocation@stpauls.us or check our internet site, www.vocationoffice.org